Miranda Mary's Write Like Me™ Series
Presents
Angel and The Little Dog

Story written and illustrated by Miranda Mary

Miranda Mary Media

LOS ANGELES ★ NEW YORK CITY ★ MONTREAL

Angel and The Little Dog First Edition Copyright 2013. Original Story and Drawings created by Miranda Mary ©2011. Text and Illustrations Copyright 2013 © Miranda Mary.

Published by Miranda Mary Media www.mirandamarymedia.com

Angel and The Little Dog and the Write Like Me Series™ are printed in the United States of America.

It is acknowledged that the main purpose of this book and the series is to encourage parents, teachers, and caretakers to use as a tool, complete with illustrations, for inspiring children to express themselves through writing and storytelling.

Book Coaching and Production Services by Stella Togo

www.TogoProductions.com

Book Cover Design, Logos and Interior Branding Illustrations designed by Tina Modugno

www.TinaModugno.com

Interior Book Layout Design by AJ Amyx

www.AJAmyx.com

Copy Editing By William Shane Tucker

Library of Congress Cataloging-in-Publication Data

Mary, Miranda

Angel and The Little Dog

ISBN-13:

978-0-615-92657-5 (Miranda Mary Media)

ISBN-10

0615926576

A Special Note from Miranda Mary's Mom and Dad with Instructions

Dear Parents,

It is our pleasure to share the stories our daughter, Miranda Mary, has written since the age of six. Miranda Mary began writing her stories in the first grade, and as a result, she has grown tremendously as a student. Writing has sparked her creativity and imagination in all aspects of her life. She has blossomed as a daughter, student and friend. It has been amazing for us, as her parents, to see her express her feelings.

With her writing and drawing, she has been able to process and overcome a variety of difficult situations from issues on the playground to the heartbreaking loss of a beloved pet. Her love of animals and storytelling has become such a big part of her life. Miranda Mary is so passionate about sharing her books and her *Write Like Me*™ *Series* with your child that we decided it would be fun to provide the pages for your child's own creation!

Please note that the first half of the book highlights Miranda's story, which you can read with your child and then guide your child to the designated pages in order to create his or her own story. We even made sure to offer a page to be used to create a front cover complete with the space for the child's name, title and drawing. Just like a grownup book, the text is designed to be on the right of the page while the drawings and illustrations are on the left. To keep things simple, you will see we've added an alphabet frame for the text pages and the theme of the book as a frame for your little one's artwork.

We feel so fortunate to have witnessed this incredible growth in our daughter, and we hope your child will learn, grow and enjoy creating his or her own stories as much as Miranda Mary. We also hope you, as parents, will treasure your child's creations as much as we do!

We invite you to visit our little Miranda Mary at www.mirandamary.com for more information.

Happy Reading, Writing and Sharing!

Heather & Jim

Miranda Mary's Dedication

For my Mom, Dad and my bestest brother for always encouraging me to follow my dreams and for telling me to always do my best and never give up.

For all children, big and small...

I hope to help you write and draw like me. Have fun creating your stories and adventures.

A Big Thank You from Miranda Mary

To Mom, Dad and my bestest brother for encouraging me to always do my best and follow my dreams

To all of my teachers, especially Mrs. Schwartz (1st Grade) for teaching me to write my first story

To Ms. Stella* for your excitement for getting my books published

To Ms. Tina* for all of your cool drawings

To Ms. Kimberlee for your encouragement

To Mr. AJ* for making my book look great and

To Miss Taylor Swift, I love listening to your music when I write my stories and songs.

To Mrs. Schild (kindergarten), I loved coming to your class every morning and pretending to be a teacher like you and teaching my classroom of stuffed animals every afternoon.

To Ms. Purcell (2nd Grade) for your excitement for teaching, writing, and for teaching me to make my writing better.

*Note: Websites of all professionals can be found in the Copyright page.

MIRANDA MARY'S

WRITE LIKE ME™ SERIES

My Favorite Animals

What Little Miranda Mary Wants You to Know

Miranda Mary is a child who has a passion for writing and animals. She began writing books in the first grade. Her dream to be a writer began innocently enough: her teacher mentioned one day to the class that if they wrote a story, the author of that story would be able to read it to the class from a large rocking chair in the front of the room—also known as the Author's Chair.

That night Miranda Mary wrote her first story. She sat in front of her class in the Author's Chair the very next day and read her story to her classmates. To her surprise, the following day brought forth many more "authors" who were ready to share their own creations. After seeing how she affected others, Miranda continued to write at a very fast pace. She would cut paper, write the story, illustrate the pictures and bind her work so that her stories would look "like the books in the stores." Miranda Mary became very passionate about teaching others to Write Like Her—and the name of her series was born.

In the two short years that followed, she has written more than twenty books to date. As she continues to write them, she has also found a passion for writing poems and songs. Miranda Mary is so excited to share her work and hopes to inspire young authors like her.

In addition to writing, Miranda Mary is very passionate about all animals. Rescuing the Blue Macaw has become a mission. Since watching the movie Rio, she has become obsessed with these magnificent birds. Her dream is to personally bring the rescued Blue Macaws to their home in Brazil and release them back into the wild. Miranda's hope is that her Write Like Me™ series will not only encourage young writers, but will also help save animals. She hopes you and your child enjoy this creative experience! Thank you for your support.

Come visit us at www.mirandamary.com to learn more!

Angel and the little dog.

By Miranda
Mary

There once was a dog who wanted a home because she stayed at a shelter that was called Animals Home. The dog's name is Angely. Angely had no home

1.

2.

But one day Angely saw a little girl walk to her cage. The little girls name was Angel. Angel looked at Angely's cute little eyes.

3.

4.

Angely was confused. She wondered what Angel asked her mom. Angel asked her mom if she could keep Angely. "Mom?" "Yes Angel." "Can I keep the dog?" asked Angel.

5.

6.

Her mom said yes. Angel smiled at Angely. Angely jumped up and down. The man that ran the shelter picked up Angely. And Angely was snuggled in Angels arms.

7.

8.

And Angely and Angel lived happily
ever after.

The End.

9.

Now it's your turn to write like me! What kind of animal would you like to have as a pet?

NAME YOUR STORY HERE:

WRITTEN AND ILLUSTRATED BY:

_____

DATE:
_____

can you draw like me?

A B C D E F G

Z

Y

X

W

V

_____

_____

_____

_____

_____

H

I

J

K

U

T S R Q P

can you write like me?

A B C D E F G

Z   H

Y   I
_____

X   J
_____

W   K
_____

V   L
_____

U   M
_____

T   S   R   Q   P   O   N

A B C D E F G

Z   H

Y   I

X   J

W   K

V   L

U _____ M

T S R Q P O N

A B C D E F G

Z   H

Y   I

X   J

_____

_____

_____

W   K

_____

V   L

_____

U   M

_____

T S R Q P O N

A B C D E F G

Z   H

Y _____ I

X _____ J

W _____ K

V _____ L

U _____ M

T S R Q P O N

To Share My Book with Your class,
School District or organization, Email Us at
Sales@MirandaMaryMedia.com
for Special Bulk Pricing.

Miranda Mary Media

LOS Angeles ★ NEW York City ★ Montreal